COOKIES

Cookies

JACQUELINE BELLEFONTAINE

JOHN BEAUFOY PUBLISHING

First published in the United Kingdom in 2011 by John Beaufoy Publishing,
11 Blenheim Court, 316 Woodstock Road, Oxford OX2 7NS, England
www.johnbeaufoy.com

10 9 8 7 6 5 4 3 2 1

ISBN 978-1-906780-46-3

Project manager: Rosemary Wilkinson
Design: Roger Hammond at bluegum
Photography: St.John Asprey
Front cover photograph: Ian Garlick
Illustration: Stephen Dew

Printed in India by Replika Press Pvt. Ltd.

RECIPE NOTES

🖎 Where milk is used in a recipe, this can be full-fat, semi-skimmed or skimmed.

🖎 All eggs are medium unless otherwise stated.

🖎 All spoon measurements are level unless otherwise stated.

🖎 Metric and imperial measurements are not always exact equivalents, so only follow one set of measurements within each recipe.

🖎 Oven temperatures have been given for conventional electric and gas ovens. For fan ovens, use the following equivalents:

Electricity °C	Electricity (fan) °C
110	90
120	100
130	110
140	120
150	130
160	140
170	150
180	160
190	170
200	180
220	200

Contents

A great place to start

If you are new to baking then making cookies is a great place to start. You only need a little equipment and there are many recipes here that are very simple to make but also a few more challenging recipes for the more experienced cook to try his or her hand. There are quick and easy drop cookies, ideal everyday treats; more involved, rolled, shaped and decorated cookies; lots of classic favourites from around the globe and even some slightly healthier cookies for those on special diets. There is something for everyone.

Is it a cookie or a biscuit? Americans tend to refer to them as cookies, the name of which comes from the Dutch word *koekje*, meaning 'little cake'. Whereas the British tend to use the word biscuit from the French *bis cuit*, which means 'twice baked'. Others choose to refer to them as cookies if they are soft, almost cake-like, and biscuits if they are crisp and brittle.

Methods of making cookies

You can divide most cookies into the following methods of making:

Drop cookies:

The quickest and easiest to make and perfect for beginners. Often made by the creaming method, the fat and sugar are beaten together, then the flour and any additional ingredients  are added and beaten until evenly combined. The mixture is soft and can be spooned or 'dropped' onto the baking sheet. Allow room for the cookies to spread during baking: the softer the mixture, the more it will spread.

Sliced cookies:

Probably the next easiest method. The dough is firm and can be shaped into a log. The biscuits are then cut at the desired thickness. The uncooked biscuit dough can be stored  in the fridge for several days and a few cookies cut and baked from the log as desired. The uncooked dough can also be frozen either pre-sliced or whole, in which case it should be left in the fridge overnight to defrost before slicing. Ideal for fresh baked biscuits everyday.

Rolled cookies:

The dough is rolled out and cut into shapes with a knife or a cookie cutter. If a dough is very soft, you may find it easier to roll out between two sheets of cling wrap. Chilling the dough

will also help. Do not add too much extra flour and try to avoid re-rolling too many times or the cookies may become tough.

Moulded cookies:

A soft dough is used and the cookies are shaped into logs, balls or crescents, with lightly floured hands. Take care not to add too much extra flour when rolling and shaping as this will

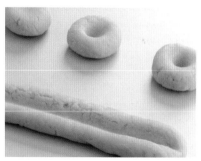

alter the careful balance of the ingredients and make the dough tough.

Piped biscuits:

Made from a dough which is soft enough to be piped from a plain or fluted nozzle to produce attractive biscuits. The consistency of the biscuit dough needs to be just right, so

very careful measuring is essential. Too stiff and the biscuits will be hard to pipe, too soft and the biscuits will lose their shape when baked.

Wafers: Probably the hardest to make as they cook very quickly so timing is critical. The mixture is very soft (a batter) and is spooned onto a baking sheet and spread out to form a circle. They are  sometimes shaped into rolls or curled. In this case you need to work fast only cooking a couple at a time, as they need to be shaped whilst warm.

Storage: Cookies should be stored in an airtight container and most will last for up to a week, many longer, unless otherwise stated in the recipe. Always store soft and crisp cookies separately or you will end up with all soft cookies. Undecorated cookies can be frozen for up to 2 months and some uncooked cookie dough can be stored for up to 1 month. Make sure cookies are completely cold before storing.

Tips for success

Oven temperature: Always preheat the oven. Cookies often cook best if cooked one sheet at a time, especially in conventional ovens with top and bottom heat. They are best cooked on the middle shelf. But if you do cook more than one sheet at a time, remember to swop the position halfway through the cooking time.

Fan ovens: These generally cook more evenly especially if cooking more than one sheet at a time, so are ideal for cookie baking but you will need to adjust the temperature according to the manufacturer's instructions, usually reducing by 10–20oC. See the chart on page 4.

Greasing baking sheets and tins: When using good quality baking sheets, you often do not need to grease them, unless otherwise stated. When required, grease lightly using a little cooking oil or butter. Over greasing may cause cookies to spread excessively and may cause the bottom of the cookies to burn.

Always use a cold baking sheet, or the cookies may spread excessively. If you need to reuse the baking sheet, allow to cool between batches.

Softened butter: Many recipes call for softened butter. If the butter is too hard it will not mix into the sugar properly. Soften butter by leaving at room temperature for 1 hour. If you forget you can soften for a few seconds in a microwave but take care: it is very easy to over soften and reduce the butter to liquid which again will not blend with the sugar properly and will make the cookies oily.

Children in the kitchen

Children often enjoy helping to make cookies and as they are relatively easy and fun, they make a good introduction to the joy of baking but do remember that a kitchen can be an unsafe environment especially for children, so NEVER leave them unsupervised.

When cooking with children, allow extra time and take extra care when putting things into and taking out of the oven, and also when using hot liquids, knives and electrical equipment.

Equipment to get you started

Scales: Accurate measuring is essential. Electronic or balance scales are more accurate than measuring cups which measure by volume and it is recommended that you invest in a set of scales if you intend to take up baking.

Measuring spoons: A set of measuring spoons is also a must for measuring ingredients. All spoon measures in books are always level unless otherwise stated.

Bowls: You will need a selection of bowls of various sizes.

Spoons: Wooden spoons are used to beat ingredients together. They can be used to beat fat and sugar together until pale and fluffy, although an electric whisk will make this job easier. For cookie making they can also be used to beat in dry ingredients, although when bringing the mixture together to form a dough, you will need to use your hands to complete the process.

Although measuring spoons must be used for measuring ingredients, a standard dessert or tablespoon can be used to spoon free-form cookies onto the baking sheets. The larger the spoon, the larger the cookie, which may take a minute or two longer to cook.

Spatula: Silicone or plastic spatulas are ideal for scraping out bowls with the minimum of waste.

Baking sheets: It is advisable to invest in a few good quality baking sheets. They will distribute heat more evenly, are less likely to twist or buckle in the oven

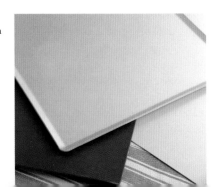

and the cookies are also less likely to stick or burn. Choose tins that feel relatively heavy and do not twist or bend easily.

Timer: Because cookies and biscuits cook quickly, you will need to keep a close eye on the baking. Times given in the recipes are a guide as ovens and the thickness and size of the cookies may vary. A timer with a loud ring is ideal to help make sure they do not overcook.

Wire racks: When cookies first come out of the oven they are often a little soft and need to be left for a minute or two to crisp up. They should then be moved to a wire rack to cool completely – the clean rack from a grill will do if you do not have a specific cooling rack. If the cookies are left to cool on the baking sheet they may stick or become soggy.

Some useful extras

Knives: A sharp knife is useful for cutting cleanly through a dough in some recipes. A rounded, flat blade palette knife is useful for transferring cookies to the cooling rack and also for spreading fillings or icings.

Electric whisks and mixers: A hand-held whisk is ideal to use in place of a wooden spoon to beat the fat and sugar together, as it is quicker and easier. Swap to a wooden spoon to beat in the dry ingredients. Also useful for whisking egg whites and batters for some cookie mixtures.

Food processor: Can be used to rub fat into flour quickly and efficiently. Also ideal for chopping or grinding nuts.

Rolling pin: You will need this when making cookies that are rolled out and cut into shapes before baking.

Cookie cutters: Use for cutting cookies into shapes before baking. They are available in many shapes and sizes and are usually made from plastic or metal. Metal cutters often have a sharper edge and give a better 'cut'. When using cutters, press down firmly, then lift off without twisting. If dough is sticky, dip the cutters in a little flour first. If you do not have any cutters, use an upturned glass.

Pastry brush: For glazes and greasing baking sheets when using oil.

Piping bags and nozzles: Required for some cookie recipes and for piping icing. Reusable and disposable piping bags and plastic or metal nozzles are available from cook shops.

Ingredients

Many cookies are made from three basic ingredients, fat, sugar and flour with the addition of other ingredients, such as chocolate, fruit and nuts, for flavour and oats, semolina, etc., for texture. The best ingredients will give the best flavour.

Fats: Butter gives the best flavour. Using salted butter eliminates the need to add salt but some recipes require unsalted butter. Use butter that is at room temperature as beating cold butter is very difficult. Baking margarine can be used but the flavour is seriously compromised and the biscuits will have a less 'melt-in-the-mouth' texture. Spreads and reduced fat spreads are not suitable. Oil is used in a few recipes. In these cases the fat does not contribute to the overall flavour, so use a lightly flavoured oil, such as sunflower or corn oil.

Sugar: Most sugar is produced from two sources: sugar cane or sugar beet. Unrefined sugars are made from sugar cane and have a higher mineral, vitamin and trace element content than refined sugars and although not essential they improve the flavour of the cookie.

The most common types of sugar used are caster, icing and light muscovado sugar (unrefined light brown sugar). It is important that the correct type of sugar is used for the best result.

Flour: Most recipes use plain or self-raising flour. If you do not have self-raising flour you can make your own by adding 2 tsp baking powder to each 225 g/8 oz plain flour. Wholemeal flour, which is flour that has been milled from the whole of the wheat grain, is used in some recipes.

Eggs: The size of eggs in baking is important. All recipes use medium-sized eggs unless otherwise stated. Remove from the fridge to come up to room temperature if possible before using, as cold eggs do not combine well with other ingredients or trap as much air.

I

everyday
treats

Makes 18
Prep time: 10 mins
Cook time: 12–15 mins

175 g/6 oz self-raising flour
75 g/3 oz butter, cut into cubes
75 g/3 oz caster sugar
1 egg, lightly beaten
6 tbsp maple syrup
approx. 18 pecan halves

Maple pecan cookies

1 Preheat the oven to 180°C/350°F/Gas 4.

2 Place the flour into a mixing bowl and add the butter. Rub in the butter with your fingertips until the mixture resembles fine breadcrumbs. Stir in the sugar. Add the egg and 4 tbsp of the maple syrup and mix until well combined.

3 Place small spoonfuls of the mixture onto baking sheets, allowing space for the cookies to spread. Push a pecan half into the centre of each one.

4 Bake for 12–15 minutes until golden. Brush the cookies with the remaining maple syrup whilst still hot, then transfer to a wire rack to cool completely.

Makes about 20

Prep time: 20 mins plus chilling

Cook time: 10–12 mins

50 g/2 oz butter, softened

50 g/2 oz caster sugar

1 egg

175 g/6 oz plain flour

a little milk

40 g/1½ oz toasted hazelnuts, finely chopped

2–3 tbsp lemon curd

Lemon and hazelnut slices

1 Beat together the butter and sugar until pale and fluffy. Beat in the egg, then beat in the flour, finally using your hands to bring the mixture together to form a soft dough. Divide the dough into 2 pieces and roll into logs about 25 cm/10 in long. Brush each log with a little milk.

2 Spread the chopped hazelnuts on a sheet of non-stick baking parchment. Place the logs on the nuts and roll to press lightly into the nuts to coat.

3 Place the logs on a lightly greased baking sheet. Flatten each log slightly. Using the handle of a wooden spoon, press a channel down the centre of each log. Fill the hollows with lemon curd. Chill for 30 minutes.

4 Preheat the oven to 190°C/375°F/Gas 5. Bake for 10–12 minutes until pale golden brown. Leave on the baking sheet until the lemon curd has set but the dough is still warm. Cut diagonally into slices and transfer to a wire rack to cool completely.

Makes about 18
Prep time: 15 mins
Cook time: 12–15 mins plus setting

100 g/4 oz butter, softened
100 g/4 oz caster sugar

1 egg, lightly beaten
75 g/3 oz plain chocolate chips
175 g/6 oz self-raising flour
3 tbsp cocoa powder
1/2 tsp chilli powder
25 g/1 oz white chocolate (optional)

Chilli choc cookies

1 Preheat the oven to 180°C/350°F/Gas 4. Lightly grease
2 or 3 baking sheets.

2 Beat the butter and sugar together until pale and fluffy,
then gradually beat in the egg. Stir in the chocolate chips.
Sift the flour, cocoa and chilli powder into the bowl and beat
together until combined to form a soft dough.

3 Place the dough on a large sheet of non-stick baking
parchment and roll out to a 30 x 20 cm/12 x 8 in rectangle.
If the dough is very soft, place another sheet of parchment on
top to make rolling easier. Cut the dough into 18 rectangles
and place on the prepared baking sheets.

4 Bake for 12–15 minutes. Allow to cool for 2–3 minutes
before transferring to a wire rack to cool completely.

5 To decorate if desired, melt the white chocolate in the
microwave or over a pan of hot water. Drizzle the white
chocolate back and forth over the cookies. Allow to set.

Makes about 16
Prep time: 15 mins
Cook time: 15–20 mins

100 g/4 oz butter
100 g/4 oz caster sugar
2 tbsp orange juice

grated zest of 1 orange
100 g/4 oz self-raising flour, sifted
100 g/4 oz rolled oats
50 g/2 oz dried cranberries, roughly chopped
25 g/1 oz chopped candied orange peel

Orange and cranberry biscuits

1 Preheat the oven to 180°C/350°F/Gas 4. Lightly grease 2 baking sheets.

2 Place the butter and sugar in a saucepan and heat gently, stirring until the butter melts and the sugar dissolves. Stir in the orange juice and zest. Remove from the heat and beat in the remaining ingredients.

3 Place dessertspoonfuls of the mixture on the baking sheets allowing space for the mixture to spread a little.

4 Bake for 15–20 minutes. Allow to cool for a minute, then transfer to a wire rack to cool completely.

Makes about 24
Prep time: 20 mins
Cook time: 10–12 mins plus setting

150 g/5 oz butter, softened
175 g/6 oz caster sugar
3 tbsp lime juice
grated zest of 1/2 lime

50 g/2 oz desiccated coconut
225 g/8 oz self-raising flour

ICING
150 g/5 oz icing sugar
1–2 tablespoons lime juice
grated zest of 1/2 lime

Lime and coconut biscuits

1 Preheat the oven to 180°C/350°F/Gas 4. Lightly grease
2 baking sheets.

2 Beat together the butter and sugar until pale and fluffy.
Beat in the lime juice, zest and coconut. Add the flour and
beat into the coconut mixture.

3 Place rounded dessertspoonfuls of the mixture well spaced
on the baking sheet. Bake for 10–12 minutes or until golden.
Allow to cool on the baking sheet for 2–3 minutes, then
transfer to a wire rack to cool completely.

4 Sift the icing sugar into a bowl and stir in the lime juice and
zest to form a smooth icing. Spread over the biscuits. Allow to
dry for 1–2 hours or until the icing sets. Store in an airtight
container for up to 5 days.

VARIATION
If time is short omit the icing, the cookies are still delicious!

Makes 16
Prep time: 15 mins
Cook time: 15–20 mins

125 g/4½ oz granulated sugar
1 tbsp dried lavender flowers

225 g/8 oz butter
225 g/8 oz plain flour
125 g/4½ oz ground rice
or semolina
caster sugar, to sprinkle (optional)

Lavender shortbreads

1 Place the sugar and lavender in a food processor and whiz for about 10 seconds. Add the butter and process until pale and fluffy. Add the flour and ground rice or semolina and whiz briefly until the dough begins to come together.

2 Tip out onto a work surface and continue bringing the mixture together to form a soft dough with your hands. Divide the dough into two. Form each piece into a ball, then roll out to form an 18 cm/7 in circle. Transfer to a baking sheet.

3 Press a fork into the edge of the circles to make a crinkled border and prick all over the surface. Mark each into 8 wedges, then chill for 30 minutes.

4 Preheat the oven to 190°C/375°F/Gas 5. Bake for 15–20 minutes until pale golden. Sprinkle with caster sugar if desired, then transfer to a wire rack to cool completely.

TIP
If you cannot find dried lavender, substitute the same amount of fresh, chopped rosemary for a similar scented biscuit.

Makes about 15
Prep time: 15 mins plus chilling
Cook time: 15–18 mins

100 g/4 oz butter, softened
50 g/2 oz icing sugar
½ tsp vanilla essence
175 g/6 oz plain flour
a little milk, if needed
fruit jam of your choice

Thumbprint cookies

1 Beat the butter and sugar until pale and fluffy, then beat in the vanilla essence. Gradually beat in the flour, bringing the mixture together to form a soft dough with your hands as you add the last of the flour. Add a little milk or water if the mixture is too dry.

2 Lightly dust your hands with flour and roll the dough into small balls about the size of a small walnut. Arranged well spaced on a baking sheet. Flatten slightly, then, using your thumb, make a deep hole in the centre of each cookie. Chill for 30 minutes.

3 Preheat the oven to 180°C/350°F/Gas 4. Bake for 10 minutes, then fill each hole with a little jam and return to the oven for 5–8 minutes until pale golden. Allow to cool on the sheet for a few minutes before transferring to a wire rack to cool completely.

VARIATION
For a chocolate thumbprint cookie: bake the cookies for 15 minutes until golden. Meanwhile, melt 50g/2 oz plain chocolate with 25 g/1 oz butter in a microwave or in a bowl over a pan of hot water. Beat in 25 g/1 oz icing sugar. Once the cookies are baked, spoon or pipe the melted chocolate into the centre of the cookies and allow to set.

Makes about 20
Prep time: 20 mins
Cook time: 15–20 mins

100 g/4 oz chopped toasted hazelnuts

2 medium egg whites

225 g/8 oz caster sugar

1 tsp cornflour

about 20 whole hazelnuts, to decorate

Hazelnut macaroons

1 Preheat the oven to 170°C/325°F/Gas 3. Line 2 baking sheets with non-stick baking parchment.

2 Place the hazelnuts in a grinder and whiz until very finely chopped. Put the egg whites in a large mixing bowl and whisk until standing in soft peaks. Gradually add half the sugar and whisk until combined and stiff peaks are formed.

3 Carefully fold in the remaining sugar, ground hazelnuts and cornflour. Place spoonfuls of the mixture well spaced on the baking sheets and press a whole hazelnut into the centre of each.

4 Cook for about 15–20 minutes until the macaroons are pale golden and can be easily removed from the paper.

TIP
Dip the base of the macaroon into melted chocolate for a special treat.

Makes about 15 small cookies

Prep time: 15 mins

Cook time: 12 – 15 mins plus setting

50 g/2 oz butter, softened

50 g/2 oz caster sugar

2 tbsp orange juice

grated zest of 1 orange

8 large basil leaves, chopped

175 g/6 oz plain flour

ICING

50 g/2 oz icing sugar

2 tsp orange juice

Orange and basil cookies

1 Preheat the oven to 180°C/350°F/Gas 4.

2 Place the butter and sugar in a mixing bowl and beat until pale and fluffy. Beat in the orange juice, zest and basil. Add the flour and beat until combined using your hands to finish bringing the mixture together.

3 Roll walnut-sized pieces of the dough into balls using lightly floured hands. Place on baking sheets, flatten slightly and bake for 12–15 minutes until pale golden. Allow to cool for a couple of minutes before transferring to a wire rack to cool completely.

4 Sift the icing sugar into a bowl and stir in the orange juice to form a smooth icing. Spread over the biscuits. Allow to dry for 1–2 hours or until the icing sets.

VARIATION

Add 25 g/1 oz candied orange peel or mixed chopped peel.

2

fancy fun

Makes about 20–40 depending on
size of cutters used
Prep time: 30 mins
Cook time: 10–12 mins plus setting

100 g/4 oz butter, softened
100 g/4 oz light muscovado sugar
225 g/8 oz plain flour
1 tbsp golden syrup

2 tbsp milk
2 tsp ground ginger (optional)

TO DECORATE
150 g/5 oz icing sugar
approx. 4 tsp tbsp water
food colouring and sprinkles
(optional)

Iced Christmas cookies

1 Preheat the oven to 190°C/375°F/Gas 5. Grease 2 baking
sheets.

2 Place the butter and sugar in a mixing bowl and beat until
light and fluffy. Add the remaining ingredients and mix to
form a soft dough.

3 Roll out the dough to 5 mm/¼ in thick and cut out
different shapes using cookie cutters. Place on the baking
sheets and bake for 10–12 minutes until crisp and golden.

4 Allow to cool on the baking sheets for 2–3 minutes, then
transfer to a wire rack to cool completely.

5 To decorate, sift the icing sugar into a bowl, stir in enough
water and mix to form a smooth icing. Colour the icing, if
desired, with a few drops of food colouring. Spread or pipe
over the biscuits and add sprinkles
if desired. Allow to dry for 1–2
hours or until the icing sets. Store
in an airtight container for up to
2 weeks.

TIP
If you want to hang the
cookies on the tree make
a hole in each cookie
with a skewer before
baking. Tie onto the tree
with ribbon threaded
through the hole.

Makes about 20
Prep time: 20 mins
Cook time: 12 mins plus setting

100 g/4 oz butter, softened
100 g/4 oz caster sugar
2 tbsp instant coffee
4 tbsp boiling water
225 g/8 oz plain flour
50 g/2 oz ground rice

FILLING
50 g/2 oz unsalted butter
175 g/6 oz icing sugar
2 tsp milk
2 tsp vanilla essence

ICING
100 g/4 oz icing sugar
1/2 tsp instant coffee
drinking chocolate or cocoa powder, to dust

Cappuccino creams

1 Preheat the oven to 180°C/350°F/Gas 4.

2 Beat together the butter and sugar until light and fluffy. Dissolve the coffee in the boiling water, then beat in. Add the flour and ground rice and mix to form a firm dough.

3 Roll out the dough on a lightly floured surface to about 3 mm/1/8 in thick, then cut into 5 cm/2 in rounds with a cookie cutter. Place on baking sheets. Repeat until all the dough is used, re-rolling as necessary.

4 Bake for 12 minutes until golden. Allow to cool for a few minutes before transferring to a wire rack to cool completely.

5 To make the filling, beat the butter until fluffy, then gradually beat in the icing sugar, milk and vanilla. Use to sandwich the biscuits together in pairs.

6 To make the icing, sift the sugar into a bowl. Dissolve the coffee in 1 tablespoon of boiling water and stir into the icing sugar until smooth. Spread over the cookies and allow to set. Dust with a little drinking chocolate or cocoa powder.

Makes about 24

Prep time: 30 mins

Cook time: 15–20 mins plus setting

1 tbsp instant coffee

2 tbsp milk

175 g/6 oz butter, softened

50 g/2 oz caster sugar

1 egg yolk

175 g/6 oz plain flour

approx. 24 walnut halves

150 g/5 oz milk or plain chocolate

Walnut whirls

1 Preheat the oven to 170°C/325°F/Gas 3. Grease 2 baking sheets.

2 Place the coffee in a small pan with the milk and heat gently, stirring until the coffee dissolves. In a mixing bowl beat together the butter and sugar until light and fluffy. Beat in the egg yolk, then the coffee mixture. Stir in the flour to form a smooth thick paste.

3 Spoon into a piping bag fitted with a large star nozzle and pipe rosettes measuring about 5 cm/2 in across onto the baking sheets. Press a walnut half gently into the centre of each.

4 Bake for 15–20 minutes or until pale golden. Allow to cool on the baking sheets for 2–3 minutes, then transfer to a wire rack to cool completely.

5 Melt the chocolate in a bowl set over a pan of gently simmering hot water or in the microwave. Place the cookies on a sheet lined with baking parchment and drizzle the chocolate over them, then leave in a cool place until set.

VARIATION

Omit the coffee and replace with 2 tsp vanilla essence instead.

Makes about 36
Prep time: 20 mins plus chilling
Cook time: 10–12 mins

150 g/5 oz butter, softened
75 g/3 oz caster sugar

1 tsp vanilla essence
5 tbsp double cream
250 g/9 oz plain flour
4 tbsp demerara sugar
1 tbsp ground cinnamon

Cinnamon twirls

1 Place the butter and sugar in a mixing bowl and beat
until pale and fluffy. Beat in the vanilla essence and 3 tbsp
of the double cream. Add the flour and mix to a smooth
soft dough.

2 Roll out the dough on a sheet of non-stick baking
parchment to form a rectangle about 30 x 20 cm/12 x 8 in.
Brush the remaining cream over the surface of the dough.
Mix together the demerara sugar and cinnamon, then
sprinkle over the cream. Roll up from the long side like a
Swiss roll. Cover and chill for 30 minutes.

3 Preheat the oven to 180°C/350°F/Gas 4. Cut the
dough into 5 mm/¼ in slices and place well spaced on
baking sheets.

4 Bake for 10–12 minutes until crisp. Cool for 2–3
minutes on the baking sheets, then transfer to a wire rack
to cool completely.

Makes about 24
Prep time: 25 mins
Cook time: 12–15 mins

175 g/6 oz plain flour
100 g/4 oz butter, cut into cubes
50 g/2 oz ground almonds
50 g/2 oz caster sugar
3 tbsp apricot jam

TOPPING
75 g/3 oz plain flour
1/2 tsp ground cinnamon
50 g/2 oz butter, cut into cubes
40 g/1 1/2 oz demerara sugar
50 g/2 oz ready-to-eat dried apricots,
finely chopped

Streusel-topped cookies

1 Preheat the oven to 180°C/350°F/Gas 4.

2 Place the flour in a mixing bowl and rub in the butter
with your fingertips until the mixture resembles fine
breadcrumbs. Stir in the almonds and sugar. Add the jam
and work the mixture together to form a smooth dough.

3 Roll out on a lightly floured work surface and cut
into 7 cm/2 1/2 in rounds with a cookie cutter. Place on
baking sheets.

4 To make the topping, sift the flour and cinnamon
into a bowl. Rub in the butter until the mixture resembles
breadcrumbs. Stir in the demerara sugar and chopped
apricots. Pile a little of the streusel mixture on top of
each cookie. Bake for 12–15 minutes or until the topping
is golden.

Makes about 24
Prep time: 30 mins plus chilling
Cook time: 10–12 mins

PLAIN CHOCOLATE LAYER
50 g/2 oz plain chocolate
50 g/2 oz butter, softened
50 g/2 oz caster sugar
150 g/5 oz plain flour
a little milk or water

WHITE CHOCOLATE LAYER
50 g/2 oz white chocolate
50 g/2 oz butter, softened
50 g/2 oz caster sugar
150 g/5 oz plain flour

MILK CHOCOLATE LAYER
50 g/2 oz milk chocolate
50 g/2 oz butter, softened
50 g/2 oz caster sugar
150 g/5 oz plain flour

Chocolate stacks

1 Break up the plain chocolate and place in a bowl over a pan of gently simmering water. Stir until melted. Allow to cool.

2 Place the butter and sugar in a mixing bowl and beat until pale and fluffy. Beat in the cooled chocolate. Add the flour and beat until combined using your hands to finish bringing the mixture together. Add a little milk or water if the mixture is too dry.

3 Repeat steps one and two twice but using first the white chocolate, then the milk.

4 Shape each of the doughs into a sausage, then flatten to form a rectangle about 5 x 25 cm/2 x 10 in long. Brush the tops of the plain and white chocolate dough with a little water to dampen. Make a stack of 3 layers, first the plain chocolate, then the white, then the milk. Chill for 20 minutes. Preheat the oven to 180°C/350°F/Gas 4.

5 Cut into about 24 slices and place on baking sheets with room for spreading. Bake for 10–12 minutes until firm. Cool for 3–4 minutes, then transfer to a wire rack to cool completely.

Makes about 20
Prep time: 15 mins
Cook time: 12–15 mins

100 g/4 oz butter, softened
50 g/2 oz caster sugar

2 tbsp milk
75 g/3 oz glacé cherries, chopped
50 g/2 oz almonds, chopped
175 g/6 oz self-raising flour
75 g/3 oz marzipan

Cherry marzipan bites

1 Preheat the oven to 180°C/350°F/Gas 4.

2 Place the butter and sugar in a mixing bowl and beat until pale and fluffy, then beat in the milk. Add the cherries, almonds and flour and mix together to form a soft dough.

3 With lightly floured hands, break off small walnut-sized pieces of the dough and roll into balls. Place on a baking sheet allowing space for the cookies to spread and flatten with a palette knife.

4 Grate the marzipan coarsely and sprinkle a little over each cookie.

5 Bake for about 12–15 minutes until pale golden. Transfer to a wire rack to cool completely.

Makes about 24
Prep time: 25 mins
Cook time: 8–10 mins

75 g/3 oz butter, softened
75 g/3 oz caster sugar
100 g/4 oz smooth peanut butter
3 tbsp golden syrup
175 g/6 oz self-raising flour
fruit jam of your choice

Peanut jelly dodgers

1 Preheat the oven to 180°C/350°F/Gas 4.

2 Beat the butter and sugar together until pale and fluffy.
Add the peanut butter and golden syrup, beating until well
combined. Add the flour and work into the mixture to
form a soft dough. Knead lightly.

3 Roll out the dough 5 mm/¼ in thick and cut out cookies
using a 5 cm/2 in round cutter. Cut out the centre of half
the cookies using a small round cutter. Re-roll these centre
cut-outs to make further cookies. Place on baking sheets,
with a little space around each. Bake for 8–10 minutes,
until pale golden. Allow to cool on the sheets for a few
minutes before transferring to a wire rack to cool
completely.

4 Spread a little jam over the whole circles and place the
rings on top.

3

the healthier cookie

Makes 10
Prep time: 15 mins
Cook time: 20 mins

1 egg
50 g/2 oz light muscovado sugar
100 g/4 oz stoned dates, chopped
50 g/2 oz dried figs, chopped
75 g/3 oz walnuts, finely chopped
50 g/2 oz wholemeal flour
1 tsp mixed spice

Date and walnut fingers

1 Preheat the oven to 180°C/350°F/Gas 4. Grease and line an 18 cm/7 in shallow, square cake tin.

2 Place the egg and sugar in a bowl and whisk until frothy and the whisk leaves a short trail when lifted from the mixture. Stir in the dates, figs and walnuts. Sift the flour and spice over the mixture and carefully fold in.

3 Spread the mixture out in the cake tin and bake for 20 minutes until firm and golden.

4 Allow to cool in the tin for 5 minutes, then cut into fingers and transfer to a wire rack to cool completely.

TIP
These cookies are high in fibre and low in fat. To save preparation time, chop the fruit and nuts in a food processor.

Makes 24
Prep time: 20 mins
Cook time: 15 mins

75 g/3 oz butter, softened
50 g/2 oz light muscovado sugar
50 g/2 oz barley malt syrup or honey
50 g/2 oz sunflower seeds
75 g/3 oz self-raising flour
75 g/3 oz wholemeal flour

Seedy wedges

1 Preheat the oven to 180°C/350°F/Gas 4.

2 Place the butter and sugar in a bowl and beat together until pale and fluffy, then beat in the malt syrup or honey. Stir in the sunflower seeds. Mix in the flours to form a soft dough.

3 Divide the dough into 2 pieces and roll each piece into a circle about 18 cm/7 in in diameter. Place on baking sheets and cut each into 12 wedges.

4 Bake for 15 minutes until golden. Allow to cool slightly, then break into wedges and transfer to a wire rack to cool completely.

TIP
Seeds are a good source of trace elements and essential oils. Try using a mixture of seeds to increase the health value of these cookies.

Makes about 40
Prep time: 15 mins plus chilling
Cook time: 8–10 mins

175 g/6 oz butter, softened
75 g/3 oz light muscovado sugar

1 egg yolk
grated zest of 1/2 lemon
2 tbsp lemon juice
1 tbsp poppy seeds
225 g/8 oz plain flour

Lemon poppy seed cookies

1 Place the butter and sugar in a bowl and beat together until pale and fluffy. Beat in the egg yolk, lemon zest and juice. Mix the poppy seeds with the flour, then beat into the butter mixture to form a soft dough.

2 Shape into a long log about 5 cm/2 in thick. Wrap the log in a sheet of non-stick baking parchment and chill until required.

3 Preheat the oven to 190°C/375°F/Gas 5. Cut 5 mm/1/4 in thick slices from the log and place on baking sheets. Leave enough space for the cookies to spread.

4 Bake for 8–10 minutes until just firm. Allow to cool on the baking sheet for a few minutes before transferring to a wire rack to cool completely.

TIP
The uncooked biscuit log can be stored in the fridge for up to 1 week or place in a polythene bag and freeze for up to 2 months.

Makes about 20
Prep time: 15 mins
Cook time: 10–12 mins

225 g/8 oz plain flour
1 tsp baking powder
1 tsp allspice

½ tsp ground cinnamon
½ tsp ground nutmeg
125 ml/4½ fl oz sunflower oil
1 egg
150 g/5 oz full-flavoured clear honey

Honey and spice cookies

1 Preheat the oven to 190°C/375°F/Gas 5. Lightly grease 2 baking sheets.

2 Place the flour, baking powder and spices in a mixing bowl and stir to combine. In another bowl, beat together the oil and the egg, then pour into the centre of the dry ingredients. Add the honey. Mix well.

3 Place spoonfuls of the mixture onto the baking sheets allowing a little space for them to spread.

4 Bake for 10–12 minutes until golden. Allow to cool for a few minutes on the baking sheets before transferring to a wire rack to cool completely.

TIP

Suitable for a dairy-free diet. You can replace the spices listed with 2 tsp of mixed spice.

Makes about 38
Prep time: 15 mins plus chilling
Cook time: 8–10 mins

175 g/6 oz butter, softened
100 g/4 oz light muscovado sugar
75 g/3 oz walnuts, very finely chopped

1 tsp dried rosemary or 2 tsp chopped fresh rosemary
175 g/6 oz plain flour
1 tsp baking powder
50 g/2 oz plain wholemeal flour

Walnut and rosemary cookies

1 Place the butter and sugar in a bowl and beat together until pale and fluffy. Add the walnuts and rosemary and mix to combine. Sift the plain flour and baking powder into the bowl, then add the wholemeal flour and mix to form a soft dough.

2 Shape into a long log about 5 cm/2 in thick. Wrap the log in a sheet of non-stick baking parchment and chill until required.

3 Preheat the oven to 190°C/375°F/Gas 5. Cut 5 mm/¼ in thick slices from the log and place on baking sheets, leaving enough space between for the cookies to spread.

4 Bake for 8–10 minutes until just firm. Allow to cool on the baking sheets for a few minutes before transferring to a wire rack to cool completely.

TIP
Walnuts are a good source of Vitamin E and essential oils.

Makes about 24
Prep time: 15 mins
Cook time: 12 mins

150 g/5 oz rolled oats
50 g/2 oz self-raising flour
100 g/4 oz ready-to-eat dried
apricots (unsulphered if possible),
chopped

50 g/2 oz unblanched almonds,
roughly chopped
75 g/3 oz light muscovado sugar
1 tbsp barley malt syrup
150 ml/5 fl oz sunflower oil

Apricot and almond cookies

1 Preheat the oven to 190°C/375°F/Gas 5. Lightly grease 2 baking sheets.

2 Place the oats, flour, apricots, almonds and sugar in a mixing bowl and stir to combine. Add the malt syrup and oil and beat into dry ingredients, making sure the syrup is well blended into the mixture.

3 Place spoonfuls of the mixture on the baking sheets.

4 Bake for 12 minutes until golden. Allow to cool slightly for a few minutes on the baking sheet before transferring to a wire rack to cool completely.

TIP
Dried apricots are a
good source of iron.

Makes 16–20
Prep time: 15 mins
Cook time: 20–25 mins

225 g/8 oz butter
150 g/5 oz dark or light muscovado sugar

2 tbsp barley malt syrup or golden syrup
500 g/1lb 2 oz rolled oats
1 Granny Smith apple, peeled, cored and chopped
50 g/2 oz dried figs, chopped

Fruity flapjacks

1 Preheat the oven to 180°C/350°F/Gas 4. Lightly grease a 30 x 20 cm/12 x 8 in square, shallow cake tin.

2 Place the butter, sugar and syrup in a small saucepan and heat gently, stirring until combined. Place the oats in a mixing bowl and stir in the apple and figs. Make a well in the centre and pour in the butter and sugar mixture. Beat until well combined.

3 Pour into the cake tin and level the surface. Bake for 20–25 minutes. Allow to cool for 5 minutes in the tin, then cut into pieces whilst still warm and transfer to a wire rack to cool completely.

TIP
Barley malt syrup is available from health food shops and contains trace elements and B vitamins.

Makes about 18
Prep time: 15 mins
Cook time: 10–15 mins

100 g/4 oz light muscovado sugar
100 g/4 oz sunflower margarine
175 g/6 oz rolled oats

50 g/2 oz plain wholemeal flour
1 piece stem ginger in syrup, chopped plus
2 tbsp of the ginger syrup from the jar
1 egg

Ginger oat cookies

1 Preheat the oven to 180°C/350°F/Gas 4. Lightly grease 2 baking sheets.

2 Place the sugar and margarine in a saucepan and heat gently, stirring until combined. Place all the remaining ingredients, except the egg, in a large mixing bowl. Beat in the sugar mixture, then add the egg and beat until all the ingredients are well combined.

3 Place rounded tablespoonfuls of the mixture onto the baking sheets. Flatten slightly with the back of the spoon.

4 Bake for 10–15 minutes until golden. Allow to cool on the baking sheet for a few minutes before transferring to a wire rack to cool completely.

TIP

Suitable for a dairy-free diet. Oats and wholemeal flour are complex carbohydrates that release energy slowly helping you to feel fuller for longer.

4

world
classics

Makes about 18 large cookies
Prep time: 15 mins
Cook time: 10–12 mins

50 g/2 oz plain chocolate
50 g/2 oz white chocolate

50 g/2 oz milk chocolate
150 g/5 oz butter, softened
150 g/5 oz caster sugar
1 egg
1 tsp vanilla extract
200 g/7 oz self-raising flour

Triple choc chip cookies

1 Preheat the oven to 190°C/375°F/Gas 5. Lightly grease 2 baking sheets.

2 Chop all the chocolate into small chunks. Beat the butter and sugar together until pale and fluffy. Beat in the egg and vanilla extract. Stir in the chocolate. Sift the flour and beat into the mixture, until well combined.

3 Place round tablespoons of the mixture onto the baking sheets leaving plenty of space around each one. Shape each mound into a round and flatten slightly with the back of a spoon.

4 Bake for 10–12 minutes until golden. Allow to cool on the baking sheets for a few minutes before transferring to a wire rack to cool completely.

TIP
The irregular
chunks of chocolate
make these biscuits
taste more
'homemade' but you
can use ready-made
chocolate chips if
you prefer.

Makes about 16
Prep time: 25 mins
Cook time: 8–10 mins

100 g/4 oz butter, softened
100 g/4 oz icing sugar
1 egg, lightly beaten
grated zest of 1/2 orange
2 tbsp orange juice

150 g/5 oz plain flour
3 tbsp cocoa powder

FILLING
50 g/2 oz unsalted butter
grated zest of 1/2 orange
100 g/4 oz icing sugar
1 tbsp orange juice

Chocolate orange creams

1 Preheat the oven to 200°C/400°F/Gas 6. Line 2 or 3 baking sheets with non-stick baking parchment.

2 Beat the butter and sugar together until light and fluffy, then gradually beat in the egg. Beat in the orange zest and juice. Sift in the flour and cocoa powder together and beat well.

3 Place the mixture in a piping bag fitted with a large star nozzle. Pipe spirals onto the baking sheets about 3 cm/1 1/4 in wide, allowing plenty of space for the cookies to spread.

4 Bake for 8–10 minutes. Allow to cool on the baking sheets for a few minutes before transferring to a wire rack to cool completely.

5 For the filling, beat the butter until soft, then beat in the orange zest and gradually beat in the icing sugar. Finally beat in the orange juice. Use to sandwich two biscuits together. Store in a cool place and eat within 2 days.

Makes about 30
Prep time: 20 mins
Cook time: 8–10 mins

275 g/10 oz plain flour
1 tsp cream of tartar
1/2 tsp bicarbonate of soda

175 g/6 oz butter, softened
225 g/8 oz caster sugar
1 large egg, lightly beaten
1 tsp vanilla essence

TO COMPLETE
1 tbsp caster sugar
2 tsp ground cinnamon

Snicker doodles

1 Preheat the oven to 200°C/400°F/Gas 6. Lightly grease 2 or 3 baking sheets.

2 Beat the butter and sugar together until pale and fluffy. Gradually beat in the egg and vanilla essence. Sieve the flour, cream of tartar and bicarbonate of soda together and beat into the butter and sugar mixture to form a soft dough.

3 Mix the sugar and cinnamon together and place in a shallow dish. With lightly floured hands, break off pieces of the dough about the size of a small walnut and roll into a ball. Roll each ball in the cinnamon mixture and place on the baking sheets allowing space for the cookies to spread.

4 Bake for about 8–10 minutes until pale golden. Transfer to a wire rack to cool completely.

TIP
Traditionally made
with cream of tartar
and bicarbonate
of soda, you can
replace these with
1 tsp baking
powder.

Makes about 20

Prep time: 20 mins plus cooling and chilling

Cook time: 10 – 12 mins

120 g/4¹/₂ oz unsalted butter

75 g/3 oz caster sugar

1 tsp vanilla essence

150 g/5 oz plain flour

Swedish butter cookies

1 Place the butter in a heavy-based saucepan and heat gently until it melts, then continue to cook until the butter turns a pale golden brown colour. Take care not to let it burn. Carefully pour the butter into a mixing bowl leaving behind the residue. Allow to cool and solidify.

2 Add the sugar to the cooled butter and beat until pale and fluffy. Beat in the vanilla, then beat in the flour and mix to form a firm dough. Form into a thick log and wrap in non-stick baking parchment. Chill for 30 minutes.

3 Preheat the oven to 190°C/375°F/Gas 5.

4 Cut the log into 3 mm/¹/₈ in thick slices and place on baking sheets. When you slice them, gently push the edges to form a round and they will re-form as they cook. Don't worry if the cookie cracks slightly. Bake for 10–12 minutes until pale golden. Allow to cool on the baking sheets for a few minutes before transferring to a wire rack to cool completely.

Makes about 24
Prep time: 15 mins
Cook time: 8–10 mins

100 g/4 oz self-raising flour
100 g/4 oz rolled oats

75 g/3 oz desiccated coconut
100 g/4 oz caster sugar
150 g/5 oz butter
1 tbsp golden syrup
1 tsp bicarbonate of soda
2 tbsp boiling water

Anzac biscuits

1 Preheat the oven to 180°C/350°F/Gas 4. Lightly grease
2 or 3 baking sheets.

2 Place the flour in a mixing bowl with the oats, coconut
and sugar and stir to combine.

3 Melt the butter with the golden syrup in a small saucepan.
Dissolve the bicarbonate of soda in the boiling water and add
to the pan. Pour over the dry ingredients and mix well.

4 Place spoonfuls of the mixture onto the baking sheets,
well spaced to allow the biscuits to spread.

5 Bake for 8–10 minutes until golden. Allow to cool for a
few minutes on the baking sheets before transferring to a
wire rack to cool completely.

Makes about 18
Prep time: 25 mins
Cook time: 15–20 mins

225 g/8 oz butter, softened
50 g/2 oz icing sugar
1 tsp vanilla essence
225 g/8 oz plain flour
25 g/1 oz cornflour

Viennese shells

1 Preheat the oven to 170°C/325°F/Gas 3.

2 Beat together the butter and sugar until pale and fluffy. Beat in the vanilla essence. Sift together the flour and cornflour and beat into the mixture. Place the mixture in a large piping bag fitted with a star nozzle.

3 Pipe small shells onto baking sheets.

4 Bake for 15–20 minutes or until pale golden. Allow to cool on the baking sheets for 2–3 minutes, then transfer to a wire rack to cool completely.

VARIATIONS
CHOCOLATE SHELLS: Melt about 150 g/5 oz milk or plain chocolate in the microwave or in a bowl over a pan of hot water. Half-dip each cooked shell in the melted chocolate. Place on sheets of non-stick baking parchment and allow to set.
CHERRY SHELLS: Decorate some or all of the shells by pressing a half glacé cherry into the cookie before baking.

Makes about 30
Prep time: 30 mins
Cook time: 20 mins

150 g/5 oz butter, softened
50 g/2 oz caster sugar

225 g/8 oz plain flour
100 g/4 oz chopped almonds, finely chopped
40 g/1½ oz granulated sugar
2 egg yolks, lightly beaten

Finnish shortbread

1 Preheat the oven to 180°C/350°F/Gas 4.

2 Beat the butter and caster sugar together until pale and fluffy. Beat in the flour and mix to a soft dough.

3 Divide the dough into 2 or 3 pieces and roll into long sausages about 1 cm/½ in thick. Cut into 5 cm/2 in lengths. Combine the nuts and granulated sugar. Dip each piece of dough into the egg yolks, then roll in the chopped nut mixture to coat. Place on baking sheets.

4 Bake for 20 minutes until golden. Cool on the baking sheets for a couple of minutes before transferring to a wire rack to cool completely.

TIP
You could use other nuts, such as chopped pecans, walnuts or hazelnuts instead of the almonds, if preferred.

Makes about 24
Prep time: 20 mins
Cook time: 10–12 mins plus setting

50 g/2 oz butter
75 g/3 oz caster sugar
2 tbsp double cream

1 tbsp plain flour
50 g/2 oz sultanas
50 g/2 oz glacé cherries, chopped
25 g/1 oz crystallized ginger, chopped
100 g/4 oz flaked almonds
100 g/4 oz milk or plain chocolate

Florentines

1 Preheat the oven to 180°C/350°F/Gas 4. Line 2 baking sheets with non-stick baking parchment.

2 Place the butter and sugar in a small pan and heat gently until the butter has melted and the sugar dissolved. Remove from the heat and stir in the cream. Stir in the flour, sultanas, cherries, ginger and almonds until well mixed.

3 Place dessertspoonfuls of the mixture onto the baking sheets allowing plenty of space for the biscuits to spread. Bake for 10–12 minutes until pale golden. While the cookies are still hot use a greased circular cookie cutter to pull the edges of the cookies in to form neat circles. Take care not to touch the mixture as it will be very hot. Allow to cool completely before removing from the sheet.

4 Place the chocolate in a bowl over a pan of hot water until melted. Allow to cool, then spread onto the backs of the Florentines. Use a fork to mark squiggles in the chocolate and allow to set.

Makes about 50
Prep time: 20 mins
Cook time: 40 mins

175 g/6 oz pistachio nuts
100 g/4 oz butter, softened
200 g/7 oz caster sugar
3 eggs

grated zest of 1 lemon
2 tbsp lemon juice
1 teaspoon aniseed (optional)
450 g/1 lb plain flour
100 g/4 oz coarse cornmeal or polenta
2 tsp baking powder

Cantucci

1 Preheat the oven to 180°C/350°F/Gas 4.

2 Roughly chop half the pistachios. Beat together the butter and sugar until pale and fluffy. Beat in the eggs one at a time. Beat in the lemon zest, juice and aniseed if using, then beat in the chopped and whole nuts.

3 Sift together the flour, cornmeal and baking powder and beat into the butter mixture, using your hands to finish bringing it together to form a soft dough. Divide the mixture into 4 pieces and roll each into a log shape about 30 cm/12 in long. Place on baking sheets and flatten slightly.

4 Bake for 30 minutes until risen and golden. Remove from the oven and allow to cool slightly. Reduce the oven temperature to 170°C/325°F/Gas 3.

5 When the logs are cool enough to handle, cut the biscuits diagonally into 1 cm/¹/₂ in slices. Place cut side down on the baking sheets and return to the oven for 10 minutes until crisp and golden.

Makes about 16
Prep time: 15 mins
Cook time: 20 mins

175 g/6 oz self-raising flour
100 g/4 oz butter
75 g/3 oz caster sugar

2 tsp ground cinnamon
1 egg, separated
2 tbsp milk
40 g/1 1/2 oz flaked almonds
1 tbsp natural sugar crystals or granulated sugar

Dutch Jan Hagel cookies

1 Preheat the oven to 180°C/350°F/Gas 4. Grease a shallow baking tin about 25 x 20 cm/10 x 8 in.

2 Place the flour in a mixing bowl. Cut the butter into pieces and add to the bowl. Rub in with your fingertips until the mixture resembles fine breadcrumbs. Stir in the sugar and cinnamon. Add the egg yolk and enough milk to bring the mixture together to form a soft dough.

3 Roll out into a rectangle that almost fits the tin. Place in the tin and press out to fit with your fingers to fill the tin completely, pressing together any cracks in the dough.

4 Brush the top of the dough with beaten egg white and sprinkle the flaked almonds over the top. Sprinkle with sugar crystals or granulated sugar and bake for about 20 minutes until golden. Cut into pieces whilst still warm and transfer to a wire rack to cool completely.

Makes about 18
Prep time: 45 mins
Cook time: 5 mins

50 g/2 oz butter
50 g/2 oz caster sugar
1 egg, lightly beaten
4 tbsp double cream
50 g/2 oz self-raising flour

Tuiles

1 Preheat the oven to 220°C/425°F/Gas 7. Lightly grease
2 baking sheets.

2 Beat the butter and sugar together until pale and fluffy.
Gradually beat in the egg and cream. Carefully fold in the
flour.

3 Place about 6 dessertspoonfuls of the batter on the
baking sheet and spread each into a 7.5 cm/3 in circle. Bake
for 5 minutes until just golden around the edges.

4 Working quickly, remove the cookies from the baking sheet
with a palette knife and drape over a rolling pin to make a
curved shape. Allow to cool.

5 Repeat with the remaining batter until all the tuiles are
made, alternating the baking sheets, so that they have time to
cool between each batch.

VARIATION
Add some finely chopped pistachio nuts or flaked almonds
to the mixture.

Recipe index